The Life and Death of Savion Cortez

The Life and Death of Savion Cortez

Rashid Darden

Old Gold Soul   Washington, DC

OLD GOLD SOUL

810 Kennedy Street NW
Suite 305
Washington, DC 20011

www.oldgoldsoul.com

www.facebook.com/rashiddarden

Copyright © 2011 by Rashid Darden All rights reserved

Printed in the United States of America. No part of this book may be used or reproduced in any manner whatsoever without written permission except in the case of brief quotations embodied in critical articles or reviews.

First Edition

ISBN 0-9765986-1-2

About Savion Cortez

Savion Cortez is a young, thoughtful, and energetic entry into the urban poetic landscape. His travels have taken him to Costa Rica, Senegal, and to London for a six-month slam poetry residency at the Royal Shakespeare Theatre.

He is a graduate of Potomac University in Washington, DC and currently resides in New York City, where he is also a teacher. He is already hard at work on his second volume of poetry.

i dedicate this moment of silence
to all those who could not tame me
i dedicate this blank space
to the parents that told you to watch out for me
i dedicate this void
to the boys who weren't men
i dedicate white noise
to identities of now and then

we spoke
soft voice hurting
deep inside
more than a sharp sword
happy hurt, stinging ears
infected by the zephyrs
of your words
so close
hearing myself
in your thoughts
so close
i live my life
on your heartbeat
sensing me in your passions
becoming your fears
we spoke

TELLING YOU

Perspective
Laying my head on the pillow
Realizing
That I've never been closer to another
Asking
Why you are so fine

Sleeping
The answer comes:
Physical characteristics
That the common man would
Note as imperfections only serve
As the means to distinguish you
From the rest of the angels
Roaming among us on the earth.

Suddenly
All of the poems are about you
Suddenly
They've always been about you
Only I never knew it
Someone…becomes you

Wonder
If this document is proof of my sincerity
Or madness
And if I am mad
Promise that I am prescribed the strongest sedative
Or lobotomize me so that I would have no recollection of you
For I would never want to think of you again
What if the brain could regenerate like the liver
Then wouldn't I be in a mess of trouble?

If the others were truly practice for my eyes,
Shouldn't I be ready for you?
How can you cause me to walk on eggshells?
You kill me so slowly and softly as a cancer

How badly I wanted to taste your lips on that night
How I would kill to know if you wanted the same
How could I have ever written a poem about another?
It was obviously just a rough draft

I could make a laundry list
Full of Why-I-Like-Yous
I won't. I promise
But you are the quintessence of my dreams
So different from me, but such my twin
A spirit must have guided me to you

Your appearance in my life has
Nullified every crush
Destroyed every notion of what being in love
Was supposed to feel like
This feeling that I have
Is probably the closest to
What?
Equilibrium
Reciprocity
I don't know
Because I don't know what you're feeling
Or what you're saying
Or who you talk to about me
If you feel for me at all
If you wish I'd just go away
And I hope not
Because I just want to touch you
Touch you
I said it
Touch you

I do glance
And imagine myself standing just molecules away from your body
My breath puffing lightly in your ear
Just want a little something, something
I want a piece…of your mind
Or just peace of mind
To know that you are thinking of me as I think of you

Damn, I haven't cried so much in months

Is your name catharsis?

be careful what you wish for, mon frère
a poem about you could turn into
something you're not ready for
like
the things i might do
if…
and when…
and if…

a poem about you would not be the
shrine to your perfection (that
you expect), but a
monument to the lust that
you can't quite comprehend

cuz i be like
damn
sometimes
and forget how to speak that proper
english that you're used to
and i be like
fuck
sometimes
when you say those little things that
make we want to walk to where you are
and rip
some things
off your body
and watch
you stand naked in front of me

be careful what you wish for…
mon frère
before you find me
ringing
your doorbell

write a poem about me
        he said
not knowing that my mansion in the sky
is wallpapered with the poems
i've already written about him

no…
he must mean
write a poem about me
and show it to me

that, i can do

UNTITLED GIFT

mist creeping underneath your door,
i materialize, fully formed
but weightless

you stir in your sleep
thinking about me
wondering about my plans
asking
question after
countless question
and recalling no straight response

the apparition of me takes shape
in the darkness
and watches you while
you dream of me

nothingness becomes rock hard
as you are straddled by
my essence

your eyelids never part
you trust the weight
that pins you down

i hover above you
hands gliding over
hands
arms
shoulders – broad

i close my eyes and
make love to you as a
blind man

lips taste:
lips
cheek
ear
forehead
chin
neck

mapping every inch and
storing each square of flesh
in my memory

we roll
and touch
and embrace
and pretzel ourselves
in sightless lust

sweat breaks simultaneously
with the dawn

rock hard nothingness dissipates

you open your eyes and
see the imprint of my essence in the air

A HAPPY POEM

i know that you will be there
in the next lifetime
when i am pokey
and you are gumby
damn it
and the world is sculpted
in psychedelic colors
by george pal
and we have adventures with
that fag hag come lately
named blue
whatever she is
and that dinosaur, too

and i will be there
the next time around
when you are ernie
and i am bert
a brilliant combination of
yellow and orange
as i eat my oatmeal
and organize my bottle caps
i wonder why you can't just
put down the duckie
if you wanna play the saxophone

and a thousand lifetimes from now
you can be the neo to my morpheus
because i'll obsess until i know that
you are the one
and trinity can stay at home

or we could be two kittens in some
old lady's house, biting and
wrestling each other

knocking over priceless knickknacks
and not giving a care because
the playful taste of your
ear in between my teeth makes
up for any damage to gertrude's
faberge eggs

or i could be smucker's
strawberry jam
spread thick and wide across
a slice of wonder bread
covering your creamy brown jif
(choosy moms choose it, you know)
melding into one entity as we are
bitten and chewed and swallowed
for digestion never felt as good
as it does when jif met smuckers

and now i don't know whether
to call you or fix
myself a sandwich

Blue Boy

The breathtaking masterpiece before my eyes,
Captivating.
This image, seared into my memory,
Is nothing short of perfection.
Divinity on canvas.
Hair like dark waters,
Skin bronzed by the Creator.
Untouchable man's hands.
Falling into your topaz eyes,
Reality slips away.
Lowering my eyes,
Closing my eyes,
I escape.

BELIEVE
(NEVER BEFORE)

when adam first got evicted and saw that nigga steve
that was you and me
where was eve?

we have been here before
yet never before

when i see you,
dreams are realized
needs are met
wants are fulfilled
fantasies materialize

we have been…

as baldwin has been
as cullen has been

you and me
believe

when i am with you,
i am one
we are we
i in i
one

your natural scent
is my aphrodisiac
your natural taste
is my feast
with you
i never thirst

i live always
in you

never before…

i thought
hoped
prayed
but when you came
you were not them
you were not him
you were you
i in i
one

believe in me…

i am he
i am not them
i am not him
we are we
i in i
one

we have been
here
before

yet
never before

HOMO ERECTUS

Explosive sensations
Redirect my thoughts
My gaze, my attention
My pheremonical instincts
To this new one
First ripples, then waves
Of fear, excitement,
And finally
Understanding
The epiphany
Causes my head to shift ever so slightly
To the door from which this…presence
Enters

Adam is his name
He walks in and
Time stands still
What on earth is this creature?
The original man, of course
All the imperfect clones of him
Were practice for my eyes
He must be the one, because now
There exists no other

i think him innocent
he rests on me
head in my chest like a newborn

he rests in the crook of my arm
not needing a pillow

he has done no misdeed
if he is innocent
then i must be guilty

Damn,
Every time I think about you
Damn,
Every time I talk about you
Damn,
Every time I walk past your door
Damn, damn, damn
Expletives pepper my vocabulary because you have rendered me senseless
Don't you know that watching you move is like my own private
Show
Me what I want to see
Sho' look good to me
I know that you know that I want to see me
In
Side
You
In
Side
Me, but,
Damn
Don't you know how good you look today, and
Damn
Don't you know that I feel this way, so
Damned
Ready every time I see you and
Damn
Can't you just come to the door naked next time so we can
Damn, damn, damn all night long
If you don't want me now
Just wait 'til after tonight
'Cause every tongue shall be untied
And every valley explored
You look good enough to eat tonight
See you at say…midnight?

I write this knowing that
if you ever see it,
it is because my heart
overruled my head,
or else I am dead.

if i got
rich and
could fly to
you
every week
end
would you
be
my man
then?

Where I belong
Is where you belong
Where we belong
Is where we are
With one another
In another place
Without roommates
And bad dreams

                                        Everything feels so right
                                        Now I just need to be
                                        Next to you and
                                        Everything's alright

If I sowed a lock
Of your hair in a field
Would armies of you
Spring forth

You walk out of the door not fully
Understanding me
But I'll see you in the morning anyway

Impure Thoughts While Walking to the Liquor Store

Pure memories can't clean my dirty head
My locs entangle more than just the dread
My scalp does capture thoughts lascivious
The memories of men mysterious
I walk away in order to be free
For crazy men are always watching me
Expecting love that's given out for naught
Remembering past loves I had forgot
My attitudes have changed, and this mindset
Peculiar, my past I should forget
But corner men cannot forget my sheets
I can't forget their smell each night I sleep

this isn't a love letter, so don't trip
this isn't a love poem, so don't flip
this isn't a game, there isn't a script
i just want you to know that i like you
now, again, still, more
and i like exactly what we are
two of an endangered species
comfortable with each other
protecting each other

the funny side:

i like what we are:
two big, mixed up
hairy animals wrestling with each other

the serious side:
i like what we are
two of an endangered species
holding each other, protecting each other
enjoying each other
forgetting the past
enjoying the present

i like knowing that you are there for me
i like holding you
i feel safe with you
i like being close to someone who is my friend
i enjoy you
i forget the past
i enjoy the present

Outer Space

The darkness
fills my mind to
shield me from the
sun beams of
your smile.

One million
and one stars
penetrate
the void.

OH, HERE IT IS

I wrote you something
But I don't know where it is
All I remember is that it didn't
Mention butterflies or flutter-by's
Or bees or roses or dandelion wine
But I think "ataraxia" was in it
That means "peace of mind"

I wrote you something
But I think I deleted it yesterday
It was an accident of course
I don't think I was Y2K compliant
It said something about your locks
And how good it feels to breathe again
And maybe a GUI thrown in for good measure

I wrote you something
But it lost its rhyme along the way
Maybe that's why I junked it
I mean, lost it, but like I said
It had some really cool words in it
I hope it finds you one day
I hope it wasn't just a passing notion

NEWNESS

I could have danced with him all night long
        and gone to bed at dawn
I could have kissed him all night long
        but his lips were just out of reach
I could have loved him all night long
        and married him in the morning

Purity of the lips and purity of the heart
        and purity of the deeds
Lead that piece of me that is connected to my body
        with an astral cord
To him, and deep inside, something feels so right

The longer I am with him, the smaller it seems I become
I am 12,
I am 8,
I am an infant,
wondering exactly what the hell is going on
For just one kiss I would move the moon
        and rearrange the stars

Right Now

So sudden, a strange thing happened
In my life now, I don't know how
I think I love him now
Riding so high on my life right now
I don't know how, just how to love him now
Can't let myself go down
But he won't always be around
So how do I ride so high right now?
Because living in the now is how I live right now
I'm making the best of now because little longer he'll be around
But I love him now anyhow

REMEMBERED CRUSH

And I dreamed of him again
We slept in this very same bed
A peaceful and content sleep
And he was,
Next to me
We faced the east and the rising sun
About to beam through my window
Our feet were bare, peeking out of the sheets
Our legs were intertwined
Like naked ivy strangling itself
His loins resting on my backside
His chiseled abdomen pressed against the small of my back
His smooth chest making contact with my shoulder blades
His strong arms encircling mine
His face resting against the nape of my neck
Our bodies become one as I awaken
To find myself alone
Without the memories of a forgotten crush
But remembering the closeness of my dream lover
And remarking:
"How odd…"

RECOGNIZE

It's something I should realize
It's nothing I can theorize
The prophecy is hard to see
It used to come so naturally
I'm writing a biography
Of two young people, you and me
It's plain to see
No fantasy
I mean that we
Should probably and naturally
Forget about the world you see
And magnify and beautify
A set of people, you and I
Secretly, I share my thoughts
Until your mind is at a loss
I'm so unkind, it blows your mind
All because of this phrase of mine
Would you like to
Play a little game with me
Or maybe read a book to me
You can see I'm your baby
Always, now, forever more
A secret's what will be in store
So recognize and realize
That I just can't apologize
For feeling freaky ways I feel
And knowing what I feel is real
That I just
Love me
Some you

the whole thing was poetic, really

before you came
it rained
and rained
so much that i had to stand inside
of a building and just watch
the water, falling from the sky,
meeting the water shooting up
from the fountain and
feeling the mist
hitting my face as the winds of the storm
blew

i was scared

i had wanted this for years
yearning for the opportunity to
touch your face
once more
to know what your heartbeat
felt like
against my chest

these waters were the years of my
tears
brought back to me by the creator
i haven't cried for your absence in so long
god needed to remind me how
far i've come

these waters were the manifestation of
my joy

i saw you after
the rains stopped
and my life was rainbows

less than 48 hours later
the storms rolled through again
through the city and
through my soul
i couldn't let it show
but i had to

we said goodbye
or maybe
"see you later"
and you showed me your two fingers
all the way down the block,
until the cab turned the corner and
i could see you no more

rain

reminding me of the gentle touch
of your fingertips
reminding me of the feel of your
lips against my flesh
reminding me of the cool taste
of your mouth

cleansing me of all mistakes
bathing me in a love eternal

the rain has
passed
and
my life will be
rainbows
once more

Slow Dance

Our bodies are illuminated by
The golden glow of the candle's flame
Contentment and serenity
To lay my head deep into your body
In that instant
Everything about you is perfect to me
Your heart beats so hard in my ear
Like a bass drum in a marching band
In your Nubian face
Dark eyes are reassuring to me
Like you're making love to me
Every time you say "Hi"
We dance
Your heart setting the slow pace
I whisper something funny that happened
Just so I can feel the laughter
Build up in your chest and
Erupt from your mouth
The noise fills my body and
Warms me up
Like a cup of hot ginseng tea
The music of your voice spills out
Over your pearly teeth
So sharp, they could easily pierce my jugular
If I allowed you to
I think I will

SKY

You and I
Sky

That's all

Sun beating like a deranged drummer
When is the last time someone touched you like that
In places not even the rain has seen
Forget everything

Just you and I
Sky

So close that nothing exists in between

MORBIDITY

I keep having fantasies of him
he has been killed in some exotic land
And I break down trying to deliver his
Eulogy

I'd drink Clorox
If I thought it would cleanse my soul
I want amnesia
So I can forget you

MELLOW BEATS

A mellow beat fades in…
Again…
And again…
I am reminded of you
The bass is your heartbeat
I close my eyes and imagine
My head against your chest
Counting each lub
And hoarding each dub

The beat fades out
And you slowly disappear
Like mist
I think of you
And try to remember the melody
That went with your bass line
But it just escapes me

LITTLE MAN

sometimes there is more to a man
than meets the eye
you are
not one of those men

i fall apart
when i hear my heart
when i remember
things that have passed
events of my life
seem so far away
but just one dream
can make everything
come back
like a stick
that's really a boomerang
bang
right on my head
those memories aren't dead
they live within me
i can smell his room
as if it were last week and not eight months ago
and i still thank god that i am not a woman
musty wood and rushing water and
shattered ego and ruined pride
and the permanent theft of romance

i fall apart
because my heart pumps
mercury through my veins
icy cold and poisonous
i cannot forget the infection
that he has given me
one in five, i think,
every time i enter a room
one in five people
have permanently frozen hearts
i fall apart
because my poisoned blood ruins my feet
so i can't walk away from
false intimacy
legs atrophy in my bed
and the blood become warm from the body
that shares my sheets
while my mind wanders

i fall apart because i have no heart
slices of it doled out to the
unwilling
unready
unworthy
until i have none left to give
and there is no something from nothing
so my love does not exist

I have hammered you out
Because I have been whited out
Ctrl, Alt, Delete
And like a freak of the week
I disappear to a time
Before you were queer
Way before I existed.
You sleep in presexual ooze
I wake you, but you hit snooze
And I am gone back on that
Lonely Greyhound track
I loved you
When mosquitoes and gnats threatened
To impregnate my naps
In manic fields of Stratfordshire
Connection reset by peer
You were never there
But I loved you when suicidal gorges
Called your made-up name

It could all be so simplex…
Wanted me to make you hard
File erase
And we were never of that place
Because I was at my Homecoming that weekend
Wasn't I?
Chillin' with my people
I never made it to Binghamton
Then Syracuse
Then Rochester
Then Ithaca
Somehow I never had the money to make the trip after all
I stayed at home and lived
Happily ever after

System will restart
File recovered
Long distance phone bone
With some Astroglide
You'll bring it home

Imagine me there
Digitized image becomes three-dimensional matter
And quite possibly, you are disappointed
Click reload
But I'm still too much at one time
Overload

I am the virus that cannot be cured
Attacking you on all levels
More than what you bargained for
I was so much more
You met your match when you met me
I am a reflection of you
You are a shadow of me
Too alike to coexist
Our meeting created a black hole
Which maybe you escaped
But I fell into
Creating nocturnal rivers for eons now
And I can only wonder
Do you swim or drown in the
Waters I conjure
Reboot

I had been studying how I may compare the prison in which you live unto mine
But as my prison is you
And your prison is your identity
I find that I am free now
I love you
But I have hammered you out

i wish you were here so that i could see you every day, take you to mcdonald's and split a fish sandwich. i would talk to you on the phone until four in the morning, or better yet, smuggle you into my house and keep you in my bed all day. i would take the metro to work with you, and wait for you until you got off. we would go to borders books & music and wander around until they closed. maybe we'd buy a book or two, but we wouldn't buy any music because we could just download it onto the computer. i wonder if you think about me at all.

STAB

pierce my flesh with the shards of your broken promises
slash at my heart with the blades of your l's
look
listen
like
love
club me with the heaviness of your lies
never, ever, forever
and when you've done all that
nail my coffin shut with the dots in your i's

i
am not the one

i
am not the one

you
might love me with all you got
but what you got is not enough
i cannot
live like this
betrayal with a kiss
from your lips
i could wonder whether you loved my
body before you loved my mind
but it doesn't matter
as the body was given up by the mind
in exchange for love
but the mind doesn't understand
(even after countless experiences)
that i can't make you love me
with my body
because my body
cant keep you

you
say you love me with all you got
but what you got just ain't enough for me
because i have inhaled those who promised me more
and i have been with ones who done me better
maybe i got entranced by your eyes
enthralled by your lies
and by the music i was hypnotized
but i hope you don't love me because
i ate you out the best
and i hope you don't love me because
you might get a poem written about you
and i'm not saying i'm stronger than you but
you don't have to worry about my blood on your hands

so
pierce my flesh with the shards of your broken promises
slash at my heart with the blades of your l's
look
listen
like
love
club me with the heaviness of your lies
never, ever, forever
and when you've done all that
nail my coffin shut with the dots in your i's

i
am not the one

i
am not the one

i
must now love you with all i got left
because all i got is the words you left me
i create my weapons
with those words
i exact my revenge
with those phrases
i lure you into the land mines of my mind
and your world evaporates into nothingness
because you forgot and slipped on my simile
and i exchange your body for your mind
because i gave up my body for your mind
but it doesn't matter
that the mind doesn't understand
because now
i have no body
now i have no mind
i am verse
and verse needs but a voice

you
cannot love me with all you got
because all you got is the shadow of a fraction of
what you think love is
and that for damn sure ain't enough
just as my body wasn't enough
to capture your mind
and your mind wasn't enough
to tame my verse
and my verse still can't change your lies
and i hope you don't remember me
because i wrote a poem about you
and i hope this doesn't make you love me
remember me because i was the voice
the unspoken word that made you say
"i wonder what he's doing now"

so
pierce my flesh with the shards of your broken promises
slash at my heart with the blades of your l's
look
listen
like
love
club me with the heaviness of your lies
never, ever, forever
and when you've done all that
nail my coffin shut with the dots in your i's

i
am not the one

i
am not the one

TELLING YOU...OFF

The silk of a spider's web was enough to suspend me
From your angular fingers
To your sharp incisors
I was
Mystified by your presence
I was
Blinded by your façade
My nonchalant attitude and ignoble goals of singular
Liaisons with multiple associates
Were destroyed
And I now recount the individuals I eschewed
Because I gave a damn about what you thought of me
And this is what happens…

A four-page epistle later
And weeks after our initial engagement
I am confused by my sudden invisibility
For now you can no longer look in my eyes
I was incognizant that
My phone calls did not have to be returned
I did not realize that I was so strong as an individual
That when I ask for your help
You do not have to offer it
And it all went downhill from there
Because this is what happens…

Shall we talk about the game?
Does this ring a bell?
    "Your appearance in my life has
    Nullified every crush
    Destroyed every notion of what being in love
    Was supposed to feel like…"
Now, what makes you think that I am a liar?

When I say that I care
I care
When I say that I want you
I want you
I suppose you missed the message
But I still feel obligated to share with you
The parts that you missed

So now is the part of the poem where I
Cast off the formalities of my language
And pick up my roots
I conjure the muses of Baraka, Brooks, and Giovanni
Because this is what happens when you piss off a poet

What were you thinking when you picked him?
He can never give you what I can
Poet versus politician, artist versus public servant
And, let's not forget
I just look better than him
Because this is what happens when you piss off a poet
Piss off a poet
Because like elephants, poets never forget
And although we may forgive
The poem lives on

Will he write you poems like me?
Will he respect you like me?
Will he offer you the world?
Will he place you above his politics?
And where can he take you?
And can he take you during the day?
And do you love him?
Do you love him?
Do you love your boyfriend now?
And if so how?
How can you love someone who can never acknowledge you in public?
And I say, this is what happens when you piss off a poet
Piss off a poet
Because a poet will love you unconditionally
But a God Damned Individual won't give a fuck

And just because I don't play your games
Don't think I've never played them
I've mastered them and moved on
You have to get played at least once to become a player
And your time is now
So player, play on
Or should I say pawn
The pawn about to get sacrificed to save the Queen
And when it happens
Pissing off a poet will be the least of your worries

I apologize for any hurt feelings
But God as my witness, you ain't gonna ever forget
What it feels like to choose the rest over the best
Because
This is what happens when you piss off a poet
Piss off a poet
Because poets don't like to be second best
And poets don't take no mess
And poets never forget
And poets use bloody tears to write their verse
And when worse comes to worse
A poet will still love your triflin' ass

fuck sleep
fuck eating
fuck working
fuck you

the floaters i see in my eyes are translucent yous

                                             no
            you will NOT be fucking me in the ass
                                       don't trip

                    anal sex is an act of power
                        that i will not give you

u no u no u no u no
i am the one who can walk down
the aisle and change your mind
interrupt your vows, your hopes, your dreams
your lies, inject myself into your life again

i
am
crazy

i was born in diana's tide
with a caul over my third eye
and my umbilical cord around my neck
i was wet
like the forests of the hesperides
i inhaled and swallowed neptune's froth
drunk with his children, i envisioned our love
underwater
an octopus crowning your head
we became one

i am touched in the head

i grew to the age of twenty-one
in as many seconds
ejaculating myself from the tide pool,
i exhaled and created you
one sliver of my thoughts yielded you
this is why i own you

i must be psycho
because i followed my visions of sameness
and conquered my fears to be with
me
you are me
because you are crazy
if we were to join, we would not cancel out
but multiply like crabs on the ocean floor
i would kill your thoughts
before i kill myself
wipe your slate clean and re-assimilate you
into my collective

i am loco

because i had a vibe

a premonition
a feeling that things were right again
but again comes the pain
look in the shallow mirror of narcissus
and see me
you cannot live without me
you are dead
you are a zombie
you cannot tame me
i own you

i am insane
because life is a plane
infinitely expanding
and you can run
but you cannot jump into the next dimension
because i created you to be inferior

i am your god
you are god-fearing
you are mortal
when i kill you
i – me – insanity
lives on

insanity is reality
your fantasy is your fallacy
i am your prophet
i am your commandment:

pray that i decide to turn back the hands of time
because i pimp the fates
i am the sheep from which they gather the wool
that they spin to thread

i hold your soul in my hand
this is why you run from me
you jump
but five brown pillars stop you

i can swallow you whole
and pass you through my system
you are more perfect as my shit

i am your last lost marble and your loosest screw
i am your garden of eden and your armageddon
i am your evil genius
i
am
you

WHY DO I STILL THINK OF YOU?

Everyone that I see in the street is suspect.
Everybody is you, from Kangol to Timbs
And everybody knows that I can't forget.
Everyone I see is him

days later, why do i think of you
weeks later, why do i think of you
months later, why do i think of you
Why do I still think of you

tentacles of his locks drag me back to the dark recesses of my past
when i was warrior enough to travel hundreds of miles for one
now i cannot leave my mind
i cannot breathe
because i try to live on the smoke from the candle's flame
i want to conjure the seven powers of Africa
because maybe they know what happened

so
much
hurt
my
cup
runneth
over

why are you still in my mind when you lobotomized yourself
you don't know me anymore
and i don't know you

THOUGH THE ROSES BEAR THORNS

seeing his
picture
was
like opening
a psychic bouquet
hurling my
mind backwards
through
time;
reliving
mistakes.

do you think about that hot night
in that magical year when
three nines became
zeroes
and
one became two
do you think about
movies
and
clichés
and
me getting lost
in college park
and finally see
ing you
and
sleeping

do you remem
ber not
calling
afterward?

do you
think
about

being the first
to do
that thing
to me?
that thing
that made
me climb
the walls?

do you remember
the dl before
jl and o?

do you
often
think of the
time that i
saw you
on the platform
at farragut north
and you pre
tended not to
know
me?

do you remember
ithaca.
when
phone
bonin'
was
in
vogue?

when you reminisce
about
him,
am i also
in that equation?
do you remember

the boy who
you loved
that lived
in the closet
and forget
the boy
who could
breathe freely
and
write you
poems?

and you.
with the brands.
both of you.
do you
remember me?

those men
i do not love.
those men
i
remember.

things are not
necessarily
made right
with
the simple
passage of time,

though i grow
through
remembrance.

those that i loved
i still love
though
the roses
that

perfume my
memory
still bear
thorns.

i bleed
for the
pieces of my
soul that
were pierced
by

lies
uncertainty
half-truths
and
the closet

and love.

of these,
the thorns
of the
red roses
were dipped
in
night
shade.

and i wonder

if i bleed
ever
ry
time
i love
again.

Also by
RASHID DARDEN

The big man on campus has a secret…

ADRIAN is handsome, brilliant, and devoted to serving others. Under the cool exterior, however, he is tormented and unfulfilled. Abandoned by his father and emotionally distant from his mother, he feels alone – adrift on campus - until he meets SAVION. With rhymes dripping from his lips like honey, Savion has just what Adrian needs: stability, maturity, and love. Although their friendship is filled with peaks and valleys, their relationship is threatened by Adrian's biggest challenge: BETA CHI PHI.

Finding the appeal of pledging his father's fraternity irresistible, Adrian decides to take the plunge and pledge Beta Chi Phi in an attempt to fill the void in his heart, even after his relationship with Savion blossoms. Almost immediately, Adrian is thrust headlong into a world of mind games, controlled behavior, and strokes from the paddle--tempered with the brotherhood that bonds men in times of adversity. Adrian knows that he must keep his relationship with Savion a secret at all costs, for if his new-found family were to learn the truth, he may have to choose…

The one he loves…or his brothers.

LAZARUS

Available again
September 2011

www.oldgoldsoul.com

Also by
RASHID DARDEN

Who will be the first to break?

ADRIAN is on a mission to heal himself from his emotional wounds. Though he is fresh off the "burning sands" of Beta Chi Phi, he suddenly finds himself alone. He sets himself to the task of reconciling with his parents while forging his own path as a newly "out" man on campus – no easy feat when some fraternity brothers still harbor animosity toward him.

ISAIAH is struggling to redefine himself. He is a student, basketball player, and boyfriend to a beautiful young lady. But who does he want to be? Isaiah's friendship with Adrian awakens new feelings within him – feelings that are both exciting and terrifying.

Over the course of one summer these two men are united as friends - and more. What happens between them is kept secret, even from their closest friends. As they cross each other's paths on the close-knit campus, they both long to finish what they started during that long, humid summer. Still, they made a promise...

COVENANT

Available
October 2011

www.oldgoldsoul.com

Also by
RASHID DARDEN

ISAIAH is head over heels in love with his boyfriend and isn't afraid to let the world know it. His unwavering love threatens his future as a professional basketball player. Though he is being forced to choose between the love of his life and his career, it appears that he could be making a decision which could irrevocably affect his future.

Meanwhile, ADRIAN has unfinished fraternity business. As a Big Brother for the first time, he has an obligation to uphold the chapter's sacred traditions, yet feels a responsibility to end the cycle of violence.

Friendships will dissolve. Rivals will return. Secrets buried in LAZARUS and maintained in COVENANT will finally explode.

EPIPHANY

Available
November 2011

www.oldgoldsoul.com

www.ingramcontent.com/pod-product-compliance
Lightning Source LLC
Chambersburg PA
CBHW072338300426
44109CB00042B/1902